Odd Fellows Encampment

Brief History and Introduction to the Degrees, Symbols, Teachings, and Organization of Patriarchal Odd Fellowship

LOUIE BLAKE SAILE SARMIENTO, J.D.

Foreword by Toby Hanson

Text Copyright © 2020 Louie Blake Saile Sarmiento

Photo and illustration Copyright © are retained by original photographers, artists and owners except those that has since passed into public domain.

Editor: Cyril Jaymes N. Plantilla
Layout and Cover Design: Louie Blake Saile Sarmiento

All rights reserved. No part of this book may be reproduced, stored in a retrieval system, or transmitted in any form or by any means, electronic, mechanical, photocopying, recording, or otherwise, without written permission of the author and copyright owners of the photos and illustrations in this book. Illegal copying and selling of publications deprive authors, publishers and booksellers of income, without which there would be no investment in new publications. You can help by reporting copyright infringements and acts of piracy to the author and publisher.

The moral right of the author has been asserted. While every effort has been made to trace the owners of copyright material reproduced herein, the author would like to apologize for any omissions and will be pleased to incorporate missing acknowledgements in any further editions.

International Research Society
on Fraternal Societies

Full Color Paperback Edition
ISBN: 978-1-7338512-7-5
Published in the U.S.A.

Contents

Foreword..i

Introduction..1

History and Origin..7

Encampment Degrees and Symbols..................13

Regalia...19

Encampment and its Officers............................25

Grand Encampment and its Officers................33

Jurisdictions...37

Membership Statistics...40

About the Author..41

Notes..43

References..48

This book is published in memory of
Brother **Donald R. Smith** (1932-2013)
Past Sovereign Grand Master of The Sovereign Grand Lodge
Independent Order of Odd Fellows

In 2009, brother Don gave me the first books I have about Odd Fellowship. Since then, we regularly communicated through e-mails and other social media platforms until his death in 2013. The books he gave helped me gather the information I needed when I started writing and publishing most of the history and information about Odd Fellowship on the internet at a time when the Odd Fellows had almost zero presence online. When I faced discouragements about the IOOF, he reminded me to remain dedicated to the principles of Odd Fellowship. He encouraged me to write and publish books as one way of educating younger generations and of helping preserve this historical fraternal organization into the future.

Foreword

It's easy to look at the state of our Encampments currently and wonder why they still exist. Too many of them have been neglected and allowed to atrophy into some kind of vestigial body where a few confused members wonder why they're having an extra lodge meeting each month but calling everything by different names. This kind of decay in our Encampments is a terrible shame. It was not that long ago that the Grand Patriarch was one of the most respected and revered figures in any jurisdiction because he presided over the branch of Odd Fellowship that was tasked with providing guidance and wise counsel to our Order.

Encampments arose from a need for learned, experienced Odd Fellows to gather together and contemplate the sublime lessons of Odd Fellowship. The founders of the Encampment branch were, indeed, the founders of Odd Fellowship in North America. Its institution grew not from a desire to emulate any other fraternity or from a need for extra meetings, but from the desire to more fully understand the teachings of Odd Fellowship. When Encampments were fulfilling their role of developing and spreading knowledge about Odd Fellowship, they were one of the most popular parts of our Order.

The Encampment branch is commonly referred to as Patriarchal Odd Fellowship because the Encampment branch was intended to mirror the role of the Patriarchs of the Old Testament. They were to be wise, learned shepherds guiding the development of the young Odd Fellows entrusted to their tutelage. Because of this idea, the Encampment degrees are rich in the symbolism of the Old Testament. My experience definitely reflected that idea. Once I joined my Encampment, I learned a lot more about the esoteric side of Odd Fellowship. That particular Encampment was very much focused on studying the history and symbolism of Odd Fellowship and provided an invaluable opportunity to learn about our Order.

In my jurisdiction, the Encampments have a couple of different functions. They bring together members from multiple lodges in a given area. They serve as opportunities to train new leaders within Odd Fellowship. They give us a place to learn about the history and symbolism of Odd Fellowship. One of my favorite things about our Encampments is they give myself and other younger members a place to sit and engage our senior members and hear the stories of the Golden Age of Odd Fellowship. Those are some of the most priceless moments of any Encampment meeting.

Today, our Encampments should still be a vital and thriving part of Odd Fellowship. Many members come to our lodges unaware of the deeper meaning of our work. Odd Fellowship has fallen behind other fraternities in the study of our history and symbolism. Far too many years have passed since the Golden Age of Fraternalism when information about Odd Fellowship was plentiful. I hope that this short book by Brother Louie Blake Sarmiento will inspire new generations of Odd Fellows to make the Patriarchal journey as I have. Our Encampments are at the heart and soul of what we do and what we believe as Odd Fellows and I hope that this book will be a catalyst to rekindle their vibrancy for the future.

Toby Hanson
Past Grand Patriarch
Grand Encampment of Washington
Independent Order of Odd Fellows

Introduction

History of Odd Fellowship

Evolving from the traditions of the guilds and journeymen associations in England nearly 300 years ago, the name Odd Fellows refers to a number of fraternal orders and friendly societies existing in more than 30 countries today. These lodges were first set up to protect and care for their members and communities at a time when there were still no social security services, national health insurance, service clubs and modern-day charity foundations. The aim was and still is to provide help to their members, their families and their communities in times of need, along with the goal of developing a sense of brotherhood and sisterhood, promoting universal peace and understanding, and improving character through the ethical and humanitarian principles taught in their ancient degrees of initiation.

Admittedly, the first Odd Fellows had "originated in obscurity

In England, the early Odd Fellows started as independent social clubs or friendly societies with moral, social and charitable purposes. These groups held their meetings and initiations inside pubs or taverns. Although the meetings and initiations were formal and involved proper decorum, this was usually followed by merry-making. The social side was often held within the same meeting room because public houses in those days were not big enough to provide a separate space for their festivities. Illustration published by Bentley and Co., 1789.

and was possibly not popular to claim any public attention of its early operations."[1] However, evidence gathered from surviving documents and recent research studies conducted by various historians and scholars suggests that the early Odd Fellows did not originate from one source. Instead, they are a result of a merger of various independent social clubs and friendly societies that existed in England at least in the middle of 17th century. Daniel Defoe in his book, *Essay on Projects*, wrote about friendly societies in 1697 and defined them as "a number of people entering into a mutual compact to help one another in case any disaster or distress fall upon them, and emphasized the contributory nature of these societies as a way to lower the poor rates and raise the self-respect of working people."[2] He recommended the creation of these societies as "a means to prevent the general misery and poverty of mankind and at once secure the country against beggars, parish poor, almshouses, and hospitals."[3] Other advocates shared the desire to use friendly societies to decrease the cost of poor relief.[4] Like cooperatives and labor unions, the members of these friendly societies would contribute some of their hard-earned wages to a common fund which they could use for unfortunate times such as sickness, losing a job or death of a member. By uniting themselves into a friendly society, ordinary workers were able to build up funds to aid each other, their families and their communities in times of need.

These early friendly societies followed the ancient usage of *self-institution*. This meant that any person can gather at least five people to form a lodge without need of approval from any national association. These lodges differed from place to place. They had rituals and customs unique to themselves and these customs evolved from time to time. They had no Grand Lodge of any kind; they were all independent and unconnected lodges. Each lodge was presided by a Noble Grand Master and governed itself according to their own rules, traditions and practices. Hence, there were actually so many clubs or lodges named "Odd Fellows" but were not formally connected with each other. They gave no benefits apart from helping widows and deceased members. The only one thing they had in common was a traveling assistance given to their members of various lodges who were traveling in search of work. If a member enters into a Lodge in another town, he is given a traveling password and a certificate to show to the lodge. He is then given assistance in terms of food and lodging. That money would then be reimbursed by one lodge to another. Unfortunately, they got into trouble in reclaiming money between lodges.

As a result, a number of these self-instituted lodges eventually decided to federate themselves into regional organizations for better administration on or before 1730. The first of these groups was presumably the *Ancient Noble Order of Odd Fellows*.[5] By 1748, there were at least nine associated Odd Fellows Lodges in England. An *Improved Order of Odd Fellows* was successively formed as a schism from an earlier organization.[6] During the mid-1700s, some lodges in southern England further split and formed the *Order of Patriotic Odd Fellows*.[7] On January 6, 1798, the Ancient Noble Order of Odd Fellows and the Order of Patriotic Odd Fellows formed a union as the *United Order of Odd Fellows*. The *Gentleman's Magazine of 1798* mentioned that the original United Order of Odd Fellows consisted of 50 associated lodges within London and its environs. However, miscommunication led some lodges in the Manchester area to declare themselves independent from the United Order in 1810 and formally organized themselves as the *Manchester Unity Independent Order of Odd Fellows* (MUIOOF) in 1813.

As an offshoot of these earlier English Orders, Washington Lodge No.1 of the *Independent Order of Odd Fellows* (IOOF) was organized in Baltimore, Maryland, on April 26, 1819 by Thomas Wildey and four Odd Fellows from England. The MUIOOF issued this lodge a dispensation as the G*rand Lodge of Maryland and the United States* on February 1, 1820. From there, the IOOF had spread throughout North America and instituted lodges in various countries around the world.

Patriarchal Odd Fellowship

The Encampment, also known as *Patriarchal Odd Fellowship,* is a higher branch of the Independent Order of Odd Fellows that confers three additional degrees to Degree of Truth or Third Degree members in good standing: *Patriarchal Degree, Golden Rule Degree* and *Royal Purple Degree*. The degree work in this branch is a result of evolution from additional degrees that were once conferred only to Past Grands (past presiding officers) of an Odd Fellows Lodge and only during sessions of Grand Lodges. In 1827, these three additional degrees were eventually bestowed in a separate branch called an *Encampment*. The degrees are based on the lessons of *Hospitality, Toleration* and

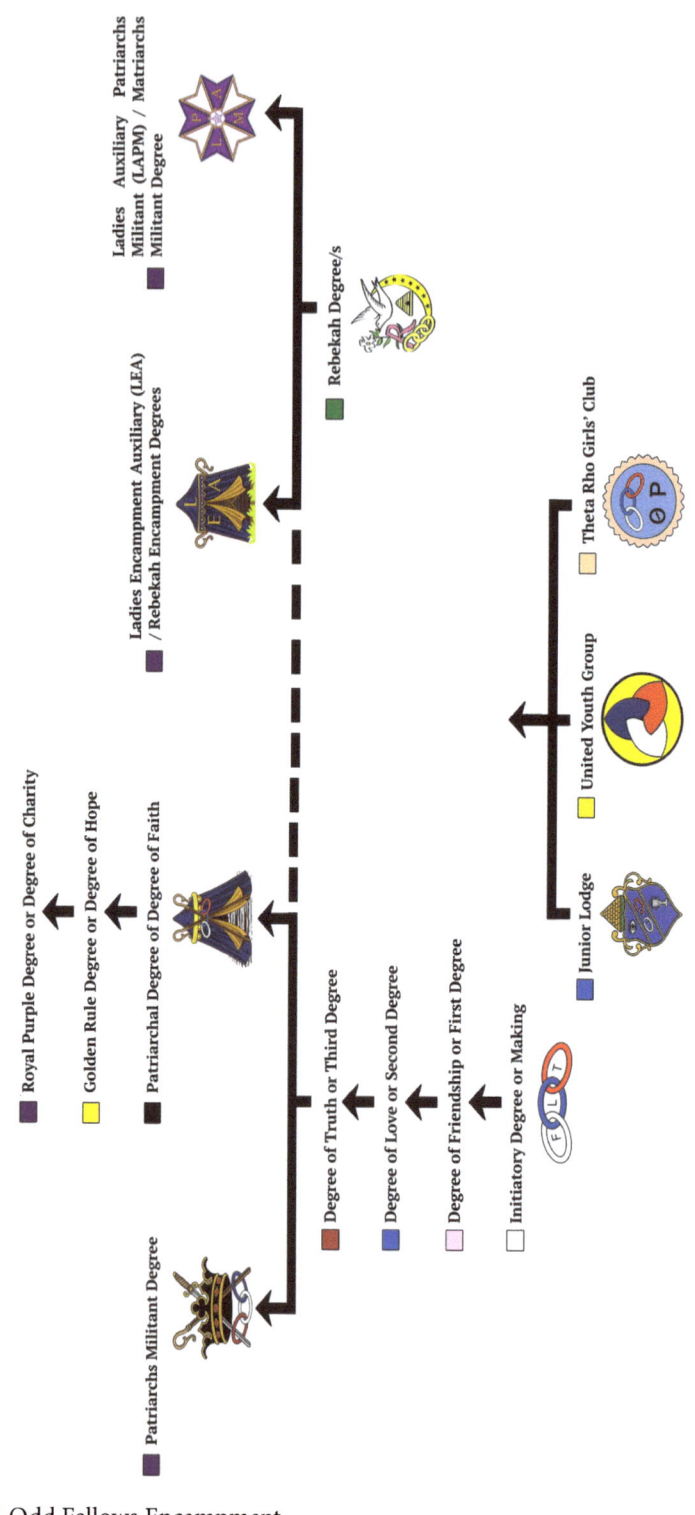

At present, the following are the degrees belonging to the different branches of the Independent Order of Odd Fellows. In Europe, however, both the Rebekah Lodge and the Rebekah Encampment have three degrees. In 2018, The Sovereign Grand Lodge lowered down the qualification for the Patriarchs Militant Degree to the Degree of Truth. Diagram by the author.

4 | Odd Fellows Encampment

Fortitude. The motto is *Faith*, *Hope*, and *Charity*.

To be eligible as a member of an Encampment, one must be a Degree of Truth or Third Degree member in good standing in his or her Lodge. The *Odd Fellows* or *Patriarchs Encampment* is traditionally for males while the females have their own branch called the *Ladies Encampment Auxiliary* or otherwise known as *Sister or Rebekah Encampment* in European jurisdictions. This was the policy during the era when most countries still implemented sex-segregation not just as a social norm but also as a law. Due to the changing gender roles and the promotion of gender equality in the 21st century, some IOOF jurisdictions have already opened the membership in the Odd Fellows Encampments to both men and women. Others have consolidated existing Odd Fellows Encampments and Ladies Encampment Auxiliaries into a *Unified Encampment,* which is open for both male and female members.

Male members are called *Patriarchs* while female members are called *Matriarchs*. The word "Patriarch" or "Matriarch" is symbolic of wisdom gained from life's experiences.[8] The title was meant to make the members visualize a very aged, white haired man or woman.[9] It

1848 illustration of a Royal Purple Degree member in full Encampment regalia. From the Collection of The Sovereign Grand Lodge, IOOF.

represents a kindly, considerate, thoughtful, experienced, patient, tolerant, and hospitable persons.[10] Persons who taught wisdom in the school of life and who have learned the important virtues from its lessons.[11] The simplicity of the Patriarchal life, the purity of faith by which the Patriarchs were guided, form a pleasing pleasure of antiquity.[12] The world today has indeed advanced in civilization and knowledge, but the heart looks back with regret at its departure from those simpler, though ruder habits of early virtue and goodness.[13] The Encampment reminds an Odd Fellow of that confiding faith and guileless simplicity.[14]

Traditionally, the Encampment is for the "most enthusiastic, the most active, the most interested leaders of the Order."[15] It was designed to be composed of selected Odd Fellows – "the most ardent of the Lodge, those who have been so impressed by the primary work and teachings of the lodge that they are impelled to advance to its higher realms."[16] Historically, the purposes of the Encampment can be summarized into the following:

- To further teach the lessons of Hospitality, Toleration and Fortitude guided by the motto: Faith, Hope, and Charity;
- To serve as unifying branch for Degree of Truth or Third Degree members belonging from different lodges;
- To provide experienced Degree of Truth or Third Degree members and past officers of the Lodge additional opportunities for personal growth and leadership development;
- To provide further understanding of the esoteric teachings and symbols of Odd Fellowship;

The peak of membership was probably in 1927 when there were 344,482 Patriarchs belonging to 3,642 Odd Fellows Encampments under 58 Grand Encampments.[17] The decline of fraternal organizations in general resulted to a substantial decrease in its numbers although there are recent signs of revival in some localities. In 2018, there are approximately 31,681 members belonging in 395 Odd Fellows Encampments[18] and 13,568 members belonging in 141 Ladies Encampment Auxiliaries (LEA)[19] or a total of 45,249 Patriarchs and Matriarchs located in the North America, Latin America, Europe, Australia, and the Philippines.

History and Origin

The Encampment as a higher branch of the Independent Order of Odd Fellows (IOOF) is distinctly North American in origin. It is best viewed as a compilation of additional degrees that were first introduced within Odd Fellowship sometime during the late 1700s to the early 1800s. Undeniably, these were first treated as Grand Lodge degrees when they were first introduced in the United States.[1]

In the United Kingdom, similar degrees were awarded to past officers based on the positions they held and their years of service in their lodge. These additional degrees were and still are being conferred by the English Orders in the District or Provincial Grand Lodge level based on merit. For example, to be eligible to receive the Purple Degree under the Manchester Unity Independent Order of Odd Fellows (MUIOOF) in the United Kingdom, a member "must have passed through the office of Past Noble Grand of a Lodge, received the four minor degrees and all the Past Lodge Officers' degrees or have served in such other offices or for such periods as their Rules prescribe

Inside the Persian Encampment room at the Odd Fellows Hall in New York. From the *Odd Fellows Family Companion*, January 3, 1852.

Early charter of an "Encampment of Patriarchs" issued to the IOOF Grand Lodge of Massachusetts on July 15, 1829. Photo by the author.

and in good standing in the books of the Lodge."[2] In that country, the Purple Degree is still conferred by the Provincial Grand Lodge only to Immediate Past Noble Grands "who have been good officers while acting in their various capacities."[3]

Undoubtedly, the original form of the Encampment degrees

originated from both England and the United States. Fragmentary records would indicate that the crude form of these degrees belonged to earlier groups. A ritual of the Loyal Ancient Order of Odd Fellows, which existed many years prior, opens a lodge in the Golden Rule Degree.[4] The ritual of the Loyal Ancient Order also referred to the *Purple Degree* and the tent emblem appeared as early as 1805.[5] The *Golden Rule Degree* was first conferred to five Past Grands in the United States by one Past Grand Larkham on February 22, 1821.[6] This was followed with the introduction of the *Royal Purple Degree* during the same year. The *Patriarchal Degree* was first conferred in the United States in 1825. They were called the "superior degrees" and were later known as the "sublime degrees."[7] Similar to the English system, these degrees were first awarded only upon Past Grands elected to membership in the *Grand Lodge of Maryland and the United States*.[8] In 1826, the Grand Lodges of Massachusetts, New York and Pennsylvania were also in possession of all these degrees.[9]

In 1827, the leaders of the IOOF decided to create a higher and select branch by grouping these three sublime degrees under a separate branch called the "Encampment."[10] Instead of being limited to Past Grands of the Grand Lodge, the membership was also opened to selected Degree of Truth or Third Degree members in good standing (also known as Scarlet Degree).[11] Legislation was proposed by Thomas Wildey and this was passed at the session of the Grand Lodge of Maryland on May 15, 1827.[12] A charter was granted to "Jerusalem Encampment No.1" on March 30, 1827.[13] On June 14, 1827, the following were duly installed as officers: John Boyd, Grand Patriarch; Thomas Wildey, High Priest; Richard Marley, Scribe; J.J. Roach, Junior Warden; and E. Wilson, Guard.[14]

On January 16, 1829, the charter was amended and reissued as of the original date for the purpose of changing the title to the "Encampment of Patriarchs."[15] This organization continued functioning under such generic designation until the *Grand Encampment of Maryland* was issued a charter on September 5, 1831, by the *Grand Lodge of the United States* (now known as The Sovereign Grand Lodge).[16] It was also during this year when the Encampment degrees were made a necessary qualification for the Representatives of the Sovereign Grand Lodge.[17]

Membership increased from 18 members in 1827 to 344,482 members belonging to 3,642 Odd Fellows Encampments under 58

Circa 1900 Encampment Degree team. From the collection of the author.

Grand Encampments in 1927.[18] The decline of fraternal organizations in general resulted to a substantial decline in the numbers. As of 2018, there are approximately 31,681 members belonging in 395 Odd Fellows Encampments[19] located in Australia, Canada, Chile, Cuba, Czech Republic, Denmark, Estonia, Finland, Germany, Iceland, Mexico, Netherlands, Norway, Poland, Philippines, Sweden, Switzerland, and United States of America.

Ladies Encampment Auxiliary

On September 20, 1851, the Independent Order of Odd Fellows became the first international fraternal organization to officially accept women when it adopted the *Rebekah Degree*. Brother Schuyler Colfax, who later became the 17th U.S. Vice President, is the author and revered founder of the Rebekahs. In 1868, the Rebekahs were given the right to vote and elect their own officers, charge for initiation fees, collect dues and undertake charitable and benevolent activities. This was way before the women's civil rights movement and before women's suffrage was even officially recognized by the U.S. Government.

For years, the Rebekah members also yearned for the adoption

Schuyler Colfax Jr. (1823-1885), 17th U.S. Vice President and founder of the Rebekah Degree, in his Past Grand and Past Chief Patriarch collar regalia. He served as High Priest of his Encampment and Representative to the Grand Lodge of the United States in 1870. Photo courtesy of The Sovereign Grand Lodge, IOOF.

of a higher branch within their organizational structure. Thus, legislation providing for the Ladies Encampment Auxiliaries (LEA) was adopted during the 1947 session of The Sovereign Grand Lodge. This branch was designed to be the Rebekah equivalent of the Odd Fellows Encampment. All Rebekahs who are wives, sisters, mothers, daughters, step-daughters or adopted daughters of members were made eligible for membership the Ladies Encampment Auxiliaries. This branch is also referred as the *Matriarchs* or *Rebekah Encampments* in European countries.

The LEA was designed at a time when sex segregation was still the prevalent societal norm. As societal norms changed in most countries, so are the rules. In 1993, Rebekah members in good standing who are under the jurisdiction of The Sovereign Grand Lodge (United States and Canada) were made eligible to join and receive the degrees of the Odd Fellows Encampment.[20] In 2001, the Sovereign Grand Lodge eventually allowed females to directly join the Odd Fellows Lodge and Odd Fellows Encampment.[21] This made the majority of Odd Fellows Encampments in the United States, Canada, Australia and the Philippines to become co-ed (open for both men and women). In European countries and Latin America, however, the Odd Fellows Encampments still remain exclusively for males while

History and Origin | 11

Official emblems of the Encampment and the Ladies Encampment Auxiliary (LEA). Courtesy of The Sovereign Grand Lodge, IOOF.

the Ladies Encampment Auxiliary or Rebekah Encampments remain exclusively for females. This is the case because both the male and female members in those countries voted to maintain the system of male-only and female-only Encampments.

But despite the fact that women are now allowed to directly join the Odd Fellows Encampments within the jurisdictions under the Sovereign Grand Lodge, the Ladies Encampment Auxiliaries and Grand Ladies Encampment Auxiliaries still exists today. The LEA is open to any Rebekah in good standing. Members are called Matriarchs and the LEA Degree is also based on the principles of Faith, Hope and Charity. As of writing, there are 13,568 matriarchs belonging to 141 Ladies Encampment Auxiliaries (LEA).[22]

Encampment Degrees and Symbols

The original Encampment degrees were purely lectures. The first printed compilation of these degrees in the United States was prepared by Thomas Wildey in 1827.[1] This ritual contained opening and closing ceremonies, and the Rules of Order. The ritual included an Initiation, Patriarchal Degree, Golden Rule Degree, Royal Purple Degree and Installation ceremonies.[2] Traditionally, not more than two degrees were allowed to be conferred on a candidate in one session, unless urgent necessity is shown.[3] Slight changes were made in the opening and closing ceremonies in 1835.[4] During this year, the designation of the presiding officer of an Encampment was referred to as Chief Patriarch instead of Grand Patriarch.[5]

In 1845, a Committee of Revision was formed composed of Past Grand Master James Ridgely of Maryland, Past Grand James McCabe of Virginia, Past Grand Sire John Kennedy of New York and Past Deputy Grand Sire William Moore of District Columbia.[6] Their revised version added dramatic elements to the degrees. The appropriate emblems and regalia were also finalized. Only one degree was allowed to be conferred on a candidate in one session.[7] The Initiation Ceremony was abolished[8] and the order of conferring the degrees was also arranged in the following: *Patriarchal Degree, Golden Rule Degree* and *Royal Purple Degree*. There was a handgrip, password, symbols, and signs for each degree.

Revisions have been made from time to time and some of the teachings from older Odd Fellows rituals were incorporated in the Encampment degrees. For example, some of the teachings found in the 1797 Revised Ritual of the Order of Patriotic Odd Fellows eventually re-appeared in the Encampment.[9] However, there is little change made in the unwritten work. Improvements in the degrees and ceremonies were again made in 1880.[10] The opening and closing ceremonies were further improved under the chairmanship of Past Grand Sire Albert S. Pinkerton in 1908.[11] Radical changes affecting all degrees were recommended and approved and this version is largely the one used today.[12] The handgrips for each Encampment degree eventually disappeared but the signs, passwords and symbols remained the same. A few years ago, the Sovereign Grand Lodge also adopted a lecture version of the Encampment Degrees as an alternative option for the use of Encampments that do not have enough numbers to perform the degrees in dramatic form. From there, only minor revisions were made.

Patriarchal Degree

The origin of this degree is unknown. Older groups such as the Grand United Order of Odd Fellows, which existed years before the IOOF, also have a higher degree called *Patriarchy*. What is known is that the earlier version of the degree that was introduced in the United States was prepared by Past District Deputy Grand Master M. Smith, a member of the Duke of Norfolk Lodge No.55 of the Manchester Unity Independent Order of Odd Fellows in England.[13] It was first presented to the Grand Lodge of the United States on September 25, 1825, by Past Grand McCormick of Maryland.[14] Its main characteristic is to test Degree of Truth or Third Degree members of their proficiency in the preceding Lodge degrees.

The main lesson of this degree is *hospitality*. Modern days have become more fictitious and misleading, it is therefore profitable to study the simple and quiet lives of the Patriarchs of the Old.[15] They dwelt mostly in tents and subsisted by raising flocks and herds.[16] They have many good virtues that have almost disappeared from present society.[17] They cultivated, to an eminent decree, the duty of hospitality, giving bread and salt to the wayfarer and stranger, after being satisfied, however, that the person is not an enemy in disguise, but a true and honest person.[18] They also had a simple but thorough trust in a Supreme Being.[19] In general, the lessons of this degree are that of hospitality and obedience and trust in the Supreme Being.[20]

In life, people will meet trials that will severely test their faith and sincerity.[21] It is told in a legion that Abraham, under the title of Aram, drove a man from his tent and out into the wilderness to suffer and to want because the man did not worship the same God.[22] However, he was reproved and required by Jehovah to call back the stranger, to entertain him, and to bear with him in his differences of opinions and practices. This degree, therefore, highlights that hospitality is to be extended to all creeds, beliefs and practices if needs be.[23] Bigotry and sectarianism must not be the field of pasture of an Odd Fellow but at their tent hospitality must be extended to the stranger of any clime.[24] A true Patriarch or Matriarch never closes his or her tent against a stranger in distress. Hospitality is not only a sacred but a pleasing duty, acknowledged such in all ages and among all nations.[25] But while it is a duty to minister to the wants of the stranger, without inquiring into his or her country, or even the cause of his or her misfortunes, it is also a duty that an Odd Fellow owes to self and family to admit no treacherous or vicious person into his or her confidence, or give that stranger the power to harm him or her or others.[26] Life, like the wilderness, will more than likely be full of questionable characters and everyone must be on his or her guard. If one is asked by those they meet, it is always the best policy to tell the truth and be sincere of his or her intentions.[27] In this degree, the Degree of Friendship is perfected by Faith. This is why this degree is also referred to as the Degree of Faith. The regalia is a *black collar* with *black lining*.

Golden Rule Degree

This degree was the first to be introduced in the United States. It was also called the "fourth degree" when it was conferred upon five Past Grands of the Grand Lodge of the Maryland and the United States, on February 22, 1821 by Past Grand William Larkam from England.[28] James Ridgely believed that this degree originated from England while others claimed that this was the work of John P. Entwisle.[29] Now that historical records are becoming more accessible, it can be inferred that the original Golden Rule Degree is English in origin. A Gold Degree already existed in older English Orders of Odd Fellows. A ritual of the Loyal Ancient Order of Odd Fellows, which existed many years prior, opens a Lodge in the *Golden Rule Degree*.[30] The parent organization of the IOOF already had a Gold Degree prior to its introduction in the United States and this degree still exists in this

English Order up to this day. However, it cannot be denied that the present Golden Rule Degree is a result of revision made by American Odd Fellows who added some literary and dramatic flavor to it. Hence, the current Golden Rule degree as we know it today is undeniable a joint-creation between the English and American Orders.

The main lesson of this degree is *toleration*. This degree teaches the cardinal virtue, the golden rule, which commands us to do unto others, as they would have them do unto us.[31] In the Encampment, no artificial distinctions of nation, sect or tribe are recognized.[32] All stand as one under one common level, and are alike entitled to that consideration and regard with each claims for himself or herself.[33] It teaches an Odd Fellow to permit others to think and act according to their convictions of duty.[34] Mankind is diverse that is why it is very impossible for everyone to think alike.[35] Humanity is composed of many races, nationalities, creeds, and customs. It has been said that religion and politics has divided mankind and had resulted to bloodshed between the Jews, Christians, Muslims and others. For how many decades, some people have tried to destroy those who differ with them. This resulted to wars that resulted to the deaths of thousands of people. Bigotry and intolerance still continue in many parts of the world today.

However, no sectarian, political and national distinctions are recognized within Odd Fellowship.[36] All are entitled to the rights which each claim for himself or herself. Odd Fellows should unite with the virtuous and good irrespective of race, country, religion, or politics in the discharge of duties which all agree are paramount to universal peace and cooperation. This degree abjures bigotry and prejudices and urges toleration toward all people of all races and creeds. It matters not "that they have different manners, customs and prejudices."[37] "All are equal, all are brethren; owning one origin, one nature, one destiny."[38] This degree is "the perfection of brotherly love in an eternal hope, so that in every human being, it matters not his or her race, color or previous condition of servitude, there are the sublimest possibilities, and as an image of the Divine he or she has the imperial right to demand due and just consideration and treatment from every man and woman."[39] In this degree, the Degree of Love is perfected by Hope. This is why this degree is also referred to as the Degree of Hope. The regalia is a *black collar* with *golden yellow lining*.

Royal Purple Degree

This degree was the second to be introduced in the United States and was called the "fifth degree", "Past Grand Degree", "Mazanin Degree", and "Purple Degree" and was first treated as a Grand Lodge Degree.[40] The original degree was presented by Thomas Wildey to the Grand Lodge of the United States on March 30, 1825.[41] It is believed that the crude form of this degree also originated from England and was subsequently revised in the United States. The ritual of the Loyal Ancient Order of Odd Fellows mentioned the *Purple Degree* and used the tent emblem as early as 1805.[42] Sublime lessons found in the 1797 Revised Ritual of the Order of Patriotic Odd Fellows can also be found in this degree. The English Orders of Odd Fellows also have their own version of a Purple Degree which was conferred only to their Past Noble Grands (past presiding officers).

The main lesson of this degree is *fortitude*. This degree, among others, teaches alertness and determination as basis for a possible success in the journey called life. Here, an Odd Fellow is taught "to see both the broad and narrow paths of life and their ultimate truths."[43] This reminds Odd Fellows that life is filled with bitter temptations, great difficulties and hotly contended struggles.[44] The uncertainties of life are always present in everyday life. Frail mortals that human beings are, we know not what a day or an hour may bring forth.[45] But human excellence is the reward of perseverance and toil in avoiding danger.[46] If an Odd Fellow will truly practice the good principles, combined with stern integrity, all will be well in his or her journey.[47] He or she will learn, and that profoundly too, how to appreciate the good that he may have done as well as what others have done and left as heritages to him or her.[48] He or she will then long to do every possible good as a blessing to the future.[49] Odd Fellows are encouraged not to be members by name only but also by deed.[50] Here, the Encampment symbols teach sublime wisdom. In this degree, the Degree of Truth is perfected by Charity. This is why this degree is also referred to as the Degree of Charity. The regalia is a *purple collar* with gold or yellow lining.

The symbols of the Encampment are the *Three Pillars, the Tent, the Pilgrim's Scrip, Sandals and Staff, the Altar of Sacrifice, the Tables of Stone, Crescent and Cross*, and *the Altar of Incense*. The esoteric meaning of these symbols according to the Independent Order of Odd Fellows are only taught and communicated upon receiving the Encampment degrees. Courtesy of The Sovereign Grand Lodge, IOOF.

Regalia

During its inception, the regalia for the Encampment was a black apron, black gloves and a collar based on the designated color of the degree received.[1] The regalia usually worn by a member of the Patriarchal Degree was a black apron, black gloves and black collar; the Golden Rule degree, the same, with black collar with gold color lace or fringe; and the Royal Purple Degree, the same, with purple collar trimmed with gold color lace or fringe, or both.[2] The black apron and black gloves disappeared at the beginning of 1878.[3]

As of now, Encampment members no longer wear aprons. Patriarchal Degree members only wear black collars or baldrics trimmed with black lace or fringe.[4] Golden Rule Degree wear black collars or baldrics trimmed with yellow lace or fringe. Royal Purple degree members wear purple collars or baldrics with yellow lace or

Circa 1840 Encampment apron and collar regalia with shepherds' staff. Photo by the author.

Cloth collar regalia

Cloth sash regalia

Encampment Rope regalia

Grand Encampment Rope regalia

Chain regalia

Velvet collar regalia

Variations of the Encampment Regalia. Photos by the author.

Past Grand and Past Chief Patriarch collar regalia. Photo by the author.

fringe. Other jurisdictions have adopted a rope version of the regalia. Some use the more modern velvet collar or chain type of regalia.

The regalia of a Past Grand of the Odd Fellows Lodge, who is also a Past Chief Patriarch of the Encampment, may, in lieu of any other regalia to which he or she may be entitled, use a scarlet collar, trimmed with white, the collar not be more than five and a half inches wide, with a roll of purple two inches, trimmed with yellow, the collar to be united in front with three links.[5]

Other jurisdictions in Canada and the United States such as California, Illinois and Washington have added the purple fez as part of the Encampment and Grand Encampment regalia in an attempt to make Patriarchal Odd Fellowship the official fez-wearing branch of the IOOF. However, the purple fez was never adopted as an official part of the Encampment regalia but its use has been liberally permitted by The Sovereign Grand Lodge until today. As of writing, the Encampment fez is confined to a few jurisdictions in North America and is not practiced by other IOOF jurisdictions in Europe, Australasia and Asia.

2012 Past Grand Patriarchs of the Grand Encampment of Illinois. Photo by the author.

The author with John Goldberg, the Grand Patriarch of the Grand Encampment of Illinois from 2012-2013. Photo by the author.

From the top: Odd Fellows Encampment officers in Sweden; Rebekah Encampment members in Sweden; and Royal Purple Degree members in Switzerland pose for a photo. Photos from the Grand Lodge of Switzerland & the Grand Lodge of Sweden, IOOF.

From the top: Candidates pose after passing through the Wilderness of Paran. New Encampments were recently instituted in Quezon City and Angeles City, Philippines.

Photo courtesy of Moses Encampment No.4, 2019 and Cabalen Encampment No.6, 2021.

Encampment and its Officers

Only members of the Degree of Truth or Third Degree in good standing in an Odd Fellow Lodge are eligible to membership in an Odd Fellows Encampment. To retain membership, the Patriarch or Matriarch must continue to be in good standing in the Lodge. In European countries, the bestowal of the Encampment Degrees is reserved to dedicated or active Third Degree members.[1] Third Degree members have to actively participate in lodge meetings and activities for at least two (2) to ten (10) years to be invited in the Encampment. In Europe, at least two (2) years is required before a member receives all his encampment degrees, and upon receiving his Royal Purple Degree, the Patriarch or Matriarch is presented an Encampment ring, nearly identical in all of the European Jurisdictions, indicating that he or she is an active and devoted member of the Independent Order of Odd Fellows.[2]

An Encampment may be organized upon receipt of a signed petition for a charter by a minimum of five (5) or more members of the Royal Purple Degree or a minimum of fifteen (15) persons of the Third Degree qualified to become members in a community within a defined jurisdiction that will in the future constitute a Grand Encampment jurisdiction, accompanied by the proper withdrawal cards and applications for membership.[3] Five (5) regular members must be maintained in good standing to keep a charter active.[4] Five (5) members in good standing in the Encampment, which is meeting, including one qualified to preside, shall constitute a quorum for the transaction of business.[5]

In the United States and Canada, Grand Encampments and Grand Ladies Encampment Auxiliaries have the power to permit the organization of *Unified Encampments* within their jurisdictions.[6] A Unified Encampment shall consist of not less than seven (7) male and female members, in any combination that includes at least two Royal Purple Degree Patriarchs or Matriarchs and at least two Matriarchs who have received the Ladies Encampment Auxiliary Degree.[7]

The elective officers of an Encampment are the following: Chief Patriarch or Chief Matriarch, High Priest or High Priestess, Senior Warden, Scribe, Financial Scribe *(if authorized)*, Treasurer, and Junior Warden.[8] To be eligible to the office of Chief Patriarch

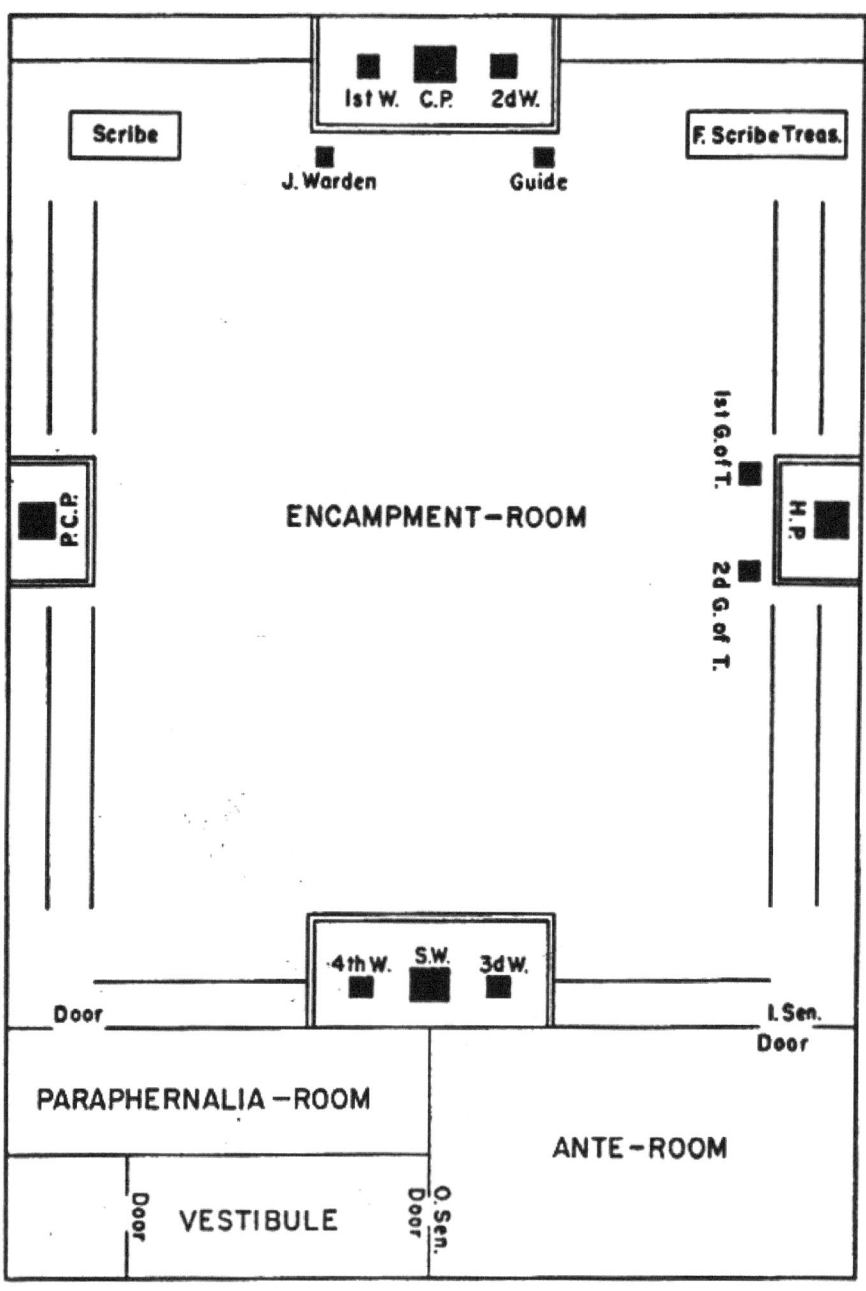

Diagram of an Encampment Room with suggested positions of officers in regular meetings. Courtesy of The Sovereign Grand Lodge, IOOF.

26 | Odd Fellows Encampment

or Chief Matriarch, one must have served a term as Senior Warden.[9] To be eligible to the Office of Senior Warden, a member must have served a term in each of two offices in the encampment. In the event there is no qualified members to hold either office, the encampment may elect any Royal Purple Degree member to be installed into the offices.[10]

The appointive officers are the following: Guide, Inside Sentinel, Outside Sentinel, First and Second Watch, appointed by the Chief Patriarch or Chief Matriarch; Third and Fourth Watch appointed by the Senior Warden; and the First and Second Guard of the Tent appointed by the High Priest or High Priestess. The Chief Patriarch or Chief Matriarch may appoint a Color Bearer and/or a Musician if the Encampment's by-laws so provide.[11]

ELECTIVE OFFICERS

Chief Patriarch or Chief Matriarch – It is his or her duty to preside over the meetings and initiations of the encampment. The regalia is a purple collar or chain with gold or yellow lining. The jewel of office is *two crossed crooks and an altar* represented or engraved within a single triangle of yellow metal.

Senior Warden – His or her duties are analogous to those of a Vice Grand of a Lodge.[1] It is the his or her duty to perform the ceremonies entrusted to him or her, and to support the Chief Patriarch or Chief Matriarch and the High Priest in the discharge of their duties. The Senior Warden presides when the Chief Patriarch or Chief Matriarch is absent. The regalia is a purple collar or chain with gold or yellow lining. The jewel of office is the *crossed crooks* stamped or engraved within a single triangle of yellow metal.

The crook, as the "staff of the shepherd," is associated with the Odd Fellows Encampment. Patriarchs and Matriarchs recognize the crook as a symbol of watchful care, which they are expected to exhibit toward other members, family, friends, and their community. Photo by the author.

Junior Warden – It is his or her duty to examine the Patriarchs or Matriarchs prior to opening; to see that the officers are at their stations; to open and close the Encampment in each degree; to assist the Chief Patriarch or Chief Matriarch and High Priest as required; and to preside in the absence of superior officers.[2] The regalia is a purple collar or chain with gold or yellow lining. The jewel of office is the *single crook* stamped or engraved within a single triangle of yellow metal.

High Priest - It is his or her duty to counsel the members of the encampment to improve themselves in the lectures and charges, as well as practice of their doctrines; to conform to the general regulations, and thus preserve the uniform mode of working in the encampment; and to give such instructions to newly admitted members as the good of the fraternity may require. He or she offers the prescribed prayers at the opening, closing and in conferring the degrees; and to instruct candidates and members in the lectures of the degrees.[3] The regalia is a purple collar or chain with gold or yellow lining. The jewel of office is the *breast plate* stamped or engraved within a single triangle of yellow metal.

Scribe – It is his or her duty to records all proceedings of the encampment. The regalia is a purple collar or chain with gold or yellow lining. The jewel of office is the *crossed pens* stamped or engraved within a single triangle of yellow metal.

Financial Scribe - It is his or her duty to keep accurate accounts between the encampment and its members; to receive all moneys due to the encampment, except when otherwise provide, and pay the same to the Treasurer at the close of each regular session, taking his or her receipt thereof. The regalia is a purple collar or chain with gold or yellow lining. The jewel of office is *crossed pens and book* stamped or engraved within a single triangle of yellow metal.

Treasurer - It is his or her duty receive from the Financial Scribe or Scribe at the close of each regular session, all moneys paid to him or her on account of the encampment and keep a true account of it; and disburse as directed by the encampment. The regalia is a purple collar or chain with gold or yellow lining. The jewel of office is the *crossed keys* stamped or engraved within a single triangle of yellow metal.

Immediate Past Chief Patriarch or Matriarch – After serving as Chief Patriarch or Chief Matriarch, a person will receive the rank and honor of a Past Grand. The regalia is a purple collar or chain with gold or yellow lining. The jewel of office is a *two crossed-crooks, a tent and the five-pointed star* represented or engraved within a single triangle of yellow metal.

APPOINTIVE OFFICERS

Guide – It is his or her duty to assist the candidates for initiation when they enter the encampment room and perform all duties assigned to him or her in conferring the degrees and otherwise, and assist the Junior Warden while in the Encampment. The regalia is a purple collar or chain with gold or yellow lining. The jewel of office is the *staff* stamped or engraved within a single triangle of yellow metal.

First, Second, Third and Fourth Watch - It is their duty to assist the Chief Patriarch or Chief Matriarch and the Senior Warden during initiation, bear their spear of office during processions or funerals and perform roles specified in the charge book. The regalia is a purple sash, collar or chain with gold or yellow lining. The jewel of office is the *spear* stamped or engraved within a single triangle of yellow metal.

First Guardian and Second Guardian of the Tent - It is their duty to act as supporters of the High Priest or Priestess' and as his or her messengers. They should always be on duty as sentinels at each side of the High Priest or Priestess' tent.[1] The regalia is a purple sash, collar or chain with gold or yellow lining. The jewel of office is the *halberd* or *axe* stamped or engraved within a single triangle of yellow metal.

Inside Sentinel - It is his or her duty to prove every Patriarch or Matriarch before he or she is admitted; to report his or her name to the Senior Warden, and by his or her direction, obtain the password of the degree in which the Encampment is open. The regalia is a purple sash, collar or chain with gold or yellow lining. The jewel of office is the *crossed swords* stamped or engraved within a single triangle of yellow.

Outside Sentinel - It is his or her duty to take charge of the anteroom, and to admit no Patriarch or Matriarch, except one with a card or official certificate, without the check password, unless directed by the Chief Patriarch or Chief Matriarch. The regalia is a purple sash, collar or chain with gold or yellow lining. The jewel of office is the *crossed swords* stamped or engraved within a single triangle of yellow.

Color Bearer - It is his or her duty, escorted by the Junior Warden and Guide, to present the flag of the country, and retire it at the close of each meeting; seeing that it is secured and cared for at all times. The regalia is a purple sash, collar or chain with gold or yellow lining. The jewel of office is the *flag* stamped or engraved within a single triangle of yellow.

Thomas Wildey, founder of the Independent Order of Odd Fellows, wearing his Encampment regalia. Courtesy of The Sovereign Grand Lodge, IOOF.

Grand Encampment and its Officers

The first Grand Encampment as the state or national governing body for the local or subordinate Encampments was established on September 5, 1831.[1] All Grand Encampments in the United States and Canada were accorded representation in The Sovereign Grand Lodge in 1841, upon precisely the same terms as Grand Lodges.[2] The Grand Encampment Degree was adopted in 1842.

An Encampment can only be chartered by The Sovereign Grand Lodge until a Grand Encampment is instituted in a State or territory.[3] When a Grand Encampment is already instituted, all the Encampments in that territory or nation shall receive instructions from, and make returns and pay percentage to their Grand Encampment only.[4] Each Grand Encampment has exclusive jurisdiction of all encampments and may exercise all power and authority not reserved by The Sovereign Grand Lodge.[5] Each Grand Encampment are also allowed to adopt its own legislation concerning minimum fees; dues and assessments, provided same shall not be lower than the minimum prescribed by The Sovereign Grand Lodge.[6] In the Europe, however, an Encampment can be instituted directly by the Grand Lodge of a particular country. This means that there are no Grand Encampments there and all Encampments within the European continent report directly to the respective Grand Lodge of that territory or nation.

Three (3) Encampments in good standing in a state, province, nation or territory may petition The Sovereign Grand Lodge for a charter to organize a Grand Encampment.[7] The petition must be on the form supplied by The Sovereign Grand Lodge signed by at least seven (7) Past Chief Patriarchs or Past Chief Matriarchs in good standing representing the three (3) Encampments and sent to the Sovereign Grand Secretary with the required fees. Only Past Chief Patriarchs or Past Chief Matriarchs in good standing in the jurisdiction and in possession of the Grand Encampment Degree may participate in or hold office in the Grand Encampment.[8]

The elective officers of a Grand Encampment are the following: Grand Patriarch or Grand Matriarch, Grand High Priest or Grand High Priestess, Grand Senior Warden, Grand Scribe, Grand Treasurer, Grand Junior Warden, and Grand Representatives. The appointive officers are the Grand Marshal, Grand Inside Sentinel, Grand Outside Sentinel, and such other officers as may be provided, who are appointed by the Grand Patriarch or Grand Matriarch. Grand Encampments may provide for the election or appointment of additional officers as needed. [9] For Grand Encampments directly under The Sovereign Grand Lodge, all elective offices may be held by either Patriarchs or Matriarchs.[10]

ELECTIVE OFFICERS

Grand Patriarch or Grand Matriarch - It is his or her duty to preside over meetings and preserve order in the Grand Encampment and make sure to execute the law and mandates of the organization. He or she also presides in instituting new Encampments, installs the officers and delivers necessary instructions on the work of the Patriarchal Order. The regalia is a purple collar or chain with gold or yellow lining. The jewel of office is the *crossed crooks and altar* stamped or engraved in the center of a double triangle of yellow metal.

Grand High Priest – It is his or her duty to open and close the Grand Encampment with a prayer, to preside in the absence of the Grand Patriarch, and to instruct members of the work of the Grand Encampment.[1] The regalia is a purple collar or chain with gold or yellow lining. The jewel of office is the *breast plate* stamped or engraved in the center of a double triangle of yellow metal.

Grand Senior Warden – It is his or her duty to assist in preserving order and enforcing the laws and rules of the Grand Encampment; to preside in the absence of the Grand Patriarch or Grand Matriarch; and to perform such duties analogous to those of the Senior Warden in an Encampment.[2] The regalia is a purple collar or chain with gold or yellow lining. The jewel of office is the *crossed crooks* stamped or engraved in the center of a double triangle of yellow metal.

Grand Junior Warden – It is his or her duty to open and close the Grand Encampment as directed; to introduce all new members; and to officiate when superior officers are absent.[3] The regalia is a purple collar or chain with gold or yellow lining. The jewel of office is the *single crook* stamped or engraved in the center of a double triangle of yellow metal.

Grand Scribe – It is his or her duty to keep an accurate account of the proceedings of the Grand Encampment, write all communications and issue all notices or summonses under the seal of the Grand Encampment. Usually, the Grand Scribe manages the office and employees of the Grand Encampment headquarters in the State, Province, nation or territory. The regalia is a purple collar or chain with gold or yellow lining. The jewel of office is the *crossed pens* stamped or engraved in the center of a double triangle of yellow metal.

Grand Treasurer – It is his or her duty to receive all monies collected by the Grand Scribe, giving receipt therefore, and deposit the same in depositories under the name of the Grand Encampment. He or she also signs all checks countersigned by the Grand Scribe or other designated signer. The regalia is a purple collar or chain with gold or yellow lining. The jewel of office is the *crossed keys* stamped or engraved in the center of a double triangle of yellow metal.

APPOINTIVE OFFICERS

Grand Marshal – It is his or her duty to assist the Grand Senior Warden in supporting the Grand Patriarch or Grand Matriarch, and to supervise the arrangements of all processions ordered or permitted by the Grand Encampment. The regalia is a purple collar, sash or chain with gold or yellow lining. The jewel of office is the *Baton* stamped or engraved in the center of a double triangle of yellow metal.

Grand Inside Sentinel - It is his or her duty to guard the inside door; to prove every Patriarch or Matriarch before he or she is admitted; to report his or her name to the Grand Senior Warden, and by his or her direction, obtain the password of the degree in which the Grand Encampment is open. The regalia is a purple collar, sash or chain with gold or yellow lining. The jewel of office is the *crossed swords* stamped or engraved in the center of a double triangle of yellow metal.

Grand Outside Sentinel - It is his or her duty to guard the outside door, and to admit no Patriarch or Matriarch, except one with a Grand Encampment Degree, unless directed by the Grand Patriarch or Grand Matriarch. The regalia is a purple collar, sash or chain with gold or yellow lining. The jewel of office is the *crossed swords* stamped or engraved in the center of a double triangle of yellow metal.

Jurisdictions

Jurisdiction	Encampment Instituted	Grand Encampment Instituted
North America (U.S.A. and Canada)		
Alaska	February 11, 1901	No Grand Encampment
Alabama	May 16, 1838	June 13, 1848
Alberta	January 11, 1887	- Data Not Available -
Arizona	July 22, 1884	August 25, 1901
Arkansas	August 31, 1847	October 14, 1875
Atlantic Provinces	- Data Not Available -	- Data Not Available -
British Columbia	January 18, 1871	March 28, 1891
California	February 1, 1853	January 8, 1855
Colorado	May 23, 1867	March 13, 1873
Connecticut	August 19, 1841	April 20, 1843
Delaware	June 20, 1831	August 2, 1848
District of Columbia	January 6, 1834	June 6, 1846
Florida	September 23, 1846	April 15, 1885
Georgia	August 16, 1843	July 12, 1847
Hawaii	February 10, 1854	No Grand Encampment
Idaho	July 10, 1876	August 6, 1888
Illinois	July 11, 1838	July 24, 1850
Indiana	October 4, 1836	January 10, 1848
Iowa	February 25, 1847	June 17, 1852
Kansas	March 14, 1859	October 9, 1866
Kentucky	August 16, 1834	November 21, 1839
Louisiana	December 24, 1832	February 10, 1848
Maine	November 7, 1843	September 13, 1845
Manitoba	May 25, 1874	October 29, 1890
Maritime Provinces	- Data Not Available -	August 9, 1892.

Maryland	May 15, 1827	December 31, 1831
Massachusetts	February 11, 1843	March 22, 1844
Michigan	April 10, 1844	February 4, 1847
Minnesota	September 1, 1851	June 7, 1871
Mississippi	April 26, 1838	January 17, 1848
Missouri	June 14, 1838	February 25, 1846
Montana	July 17, 1872	November 18, 1883
Nebraska	May 3, 1862	July 1, 1872
New Hampshire	May 9, 1844	October 28, 1845
New Jersey	July 4, 1833	May 11, 1843
New Mexico	March 8, 1853	- Data Not Available -
New York	June 25, 1829	August 18, 1839
Nevada	July 17, 1864	March 2, 1875
North Carolina	January 5, 1843	July 16, 1847
North Dakota	- Data Not Available -	May 21, 1890
Ohio	December 7, 1832	September 24, 1839
Oklahoma	August 27, 1891	April 27, 1893
Ontario	September 17, 1845	May 31, 1869
Oregon	September 25, 1857	March 29, 1875
Pennsylvania	September 7, 1828	June 17, 1829
Quebec	November 6, 1874	April 16, 1909
Rhode Island	April 9, 1844	July 11, 1849
Saskatchewan	- Data Not Available -	- Data Not Available -
South Carolina	February 21, 1842	August 11, 1843
South Dakota	May 24, 1874	August 10, 1881
Tennessee	December 20, 1842	July 21, 1847
Texas	November 23, 1847	December 5, 1853
Utah	July 15, 1873	February 22, 1888
Vermont	July 14, 1846	June 21, 1871
Virginia	January 11, 1836	November 15, 1842
Washington	April 14, 1875	May 14, 1884
West Virginia	January 11, 1836	December 5, 1865
Wisconsin	August 4, 1838	March 8, 1849
Wyoming	September _, 1870	November 29, 1881

	Latin America	
Chile	November 18, 1875	No Grand Encampment
Cuba	March 5, 1924	June __, 1942
Mexico	June 18, 1888	No Grand Encampment
Peru	September 22, 1876	No Grand Encampment
	Europe	
Austria	June 3, 1932	Encampments in Europe directly report to its own Grand Lodges.
Belgium	- Data Not Available -	
Czech Republic	- Data Not Available -	
Denmark	July 1, 1881	
Estonia	- Data Not Available -	
Finland	May 9, 1952	
Germany	May 23, 1871	
Iceland	- Data Not Available -	
Italy	- Data Not Available -	
Netherlands	September 9, 1922	
Norway	November 2, 1919	
Poland	May 8, 2010	
Sweden	October 12, 1891	
Switzerland	May 6, 1888	
	Asia and the Pacific	
Australia	October 28, 1868	June 18, 1869
New Zealand	- Data Not Available -	- Data Not Available -
Philippines	June 12, 1912 / November 21, 2009	Encampments directly report to its own Grand Lodge and The Sovereign Grand Lodge.

Membership Statistics

Year	Number of Encampments	Membership
1827	1	18
1840	34	834
1850	499	19,722
1860	671	23,674
1870	1,059	56,390
1880	1,829	86,701
1890	2,091	119,462
1900	2,669	134,805
1910	3,687	221,497
1920	3,500	318,332
1930	3,319	257,883
1940	2,527	111,753
1950	2,285	131,222
1960	2,058	95,753
1970	1,679	71,807
1980	1,245	57,225
1990-	946	47,135
2000	736	40,224
2010	534	35,395
2018	395	31,110

About the Author

Louie Blake Saile Sarmiento finished his Associate in Health Science Education in 2007; Bachelor of Science in Psychology with Certificate in Human Resource Management and Certificate in Women's Studies in 2010; Master of Arts in Industrial/Organizational Psychology in 2013; and Juris Doctor (law) degree in 2020. With a wide range of academic backgrounds, he uses various quantitative and qualitative research methodologies in his writings. He does not rely solely on old history books and manuals written many years ago but also conducts interviews, surveys, SWOT analysis, case studies and consults the most recent dissertations, thesis and expert opinions of historians, sociologists, psychologists, lawyers and other academic scholars.

He is instrumental in re-establishing Odd Fellowship in the Philippines. He is a Past Grand and Past District Deputy Sovereign Grand Master of the Independent Order of Odd Fellows. He is credited for connecting thousands of members from various countries when he created and managed the first social media groups and pages of the Independent Order of Odd Fellows from 2009-2019. He is also credited for writing and creating most of the modern literature and infographics about Odd Fellowship on the internet at a time when the organization had almost zero presence online, including the first YouTube videos and the Wikipedia entries about the Odd Fellows. Because of his contributions, he was appointed as Public Relations Coordinator and member of both the Communications Committee and the Revitalization Committee of the Sovereign Grand Lodge from 2012-2015. He was based at the Odd Fellows International Headquarters in North Carolina for an aggregate period of three years where he had full access and was able to read from cover-to-cover all available journals, history books, manuals, rituals and secret works of the Odd Fellows. He traveled widely for more than six years to conduct research and case studies about Odd Fellowship and similar fraternal organizations; visited over a hundred Lodges and several Grand Lodges across the United States and Canada; read and reviewed volumes of records, books and artifacts; observed meetings and initiations; and interviewed local, national and international leaders.

He is an advocate for the preservation of historical fraternal organizations, service clubs and civic associations. He is a member of all branches of the Independent Order of Odd Fellows (IOOF), including the Rebekah Lodge, Encampment and Patriarchs Militant. He is also affiliated with the Grand United Order of Odd Fellows (GUOOF); Ancient Mystic Order of Samaritans (AMOS); Noble Order of Muscovites (Muscovites); International Order of DeMolay (IOD); International Order of Free Gardeners (IOFG); Universal Druid Order (UDO); Ordo Supremus Militaris Templi Hierosolymitani - Regency (OSMTH); Knights of Rizal (KOR); The Fraternal Order of Eagles - Philippine Eagles (TFOE-PE); and Tau Gamma Phi or Triskelion Grand Fraternity (TGP). He now enjoys living a secluded and peaceful life while focusing on his career. As a hobby, he writes and collects books, antiques and artifacts related to fraternal organizations, service clubs and other civic associations.

Other Books by the Author

Title: Odd Fellows - Rediscovering More Than 200 Years of History, Traditions and Community Service

Publication date: April 26, 2019 (Last updated December 4, 2020)

Title: Ancient Rites of Odd Fellowship - Revisiting the Revised Ritual of the Order of Patriotic Odd Fellows, 1797

Publication date: September 30, 2020

Title: Odd Fellows Manual: Modern Guide to the Origin, History, Rituals, Symbols and Organization of the Independent Order of Odd Fellows

Publication date: December 3, 2020

Notes

I. Introduction

1. Henry Stillson, *The Official History of Odd Fellowship: The Three Link Fraternity*, 21.
2. Daniel Defoe, *Essay on Projects*, published in 1697.
3. Ibid.
4. Simon Cordery, *British Friendly Societies, 1750-1914*, Palgrave Macmillan, New York.
5. Henry Stillson, *The Official History of Odd Fellowship: The Three Link Fraternity*, 739.
6. Ibid.
7. Ibid.
8. Nathan Billstein, A Brief History of The Encampment Branch of the I.O.O.F. and A Statement of Its Accomplishments and Aims, 16.
9. Nathan Billstein, A Brief History of The Encampment Branch of the I.O.O.F. and A Statement of Its Accomplishments and Aims, 16.
10. Ibid.
11. Ibid.
12. Rev. A.B. Grosh, The Odd Fellows Manual, 275.
13. Ibid.
14. Ibid.
15. Nathan Billstein, A Brief History of The Encampment Branch of the I.O.O.F. and A Statement of Its Accomplishments and Aims, 16-19.
16. Ibid.
17. Annual Report of Grand Encampments to The Sovereign Grand Lodge, I.O.O.F ending December 31, 1927.
18. Annual Report of Grand Encampments to The Sovereign Grand Lodge, I.O.O.F ending December 31, 2018.
19. Annual Report of Grand Ladies Encampment Auxiliaries to The Sovereign Grand Lodge, I.O.O.F ending December 31, 2018.

II. History

1. Rev. Benson Mahlon Powell, The Triple Links, 195.
2. Ritual of the Independent Order of Odd Fellows Manchester Unity Friendly Society, 121.
3. Ibid.
4. Powley, Concise History of Odd Fellowship, 35.
5. Ibid.

6. Ibid.
7. Nathan Billstein, A Brief History of The Encampment Branch of the I.O.O.F. and A Statement of Its Accomplishents and Aims, 6.
8. Ibid.
9. Rev. Benson Mahlon Powell, The Triple Links, 198.
10. Nathan Billstein, A Brief History of The Encampment Branch of the I.O.O.F. and A Statement of Its Accomplishments and Aims, 6.
11. Ibid, 7.
12. Ibid.
13. Ibid.
14. Ibid.
15. Ibid.
16. Ibid.
17. Ibid.
18. Nathan Billstein, A Brief History of The Encampment Branch of the I.O.O.F. and a Statement of Its Accomplishments and Aims, 19.
19. Advance Reports of the Officers and Committees of The Sovereign Grand Lodge Independent Order of Odd Fellows Held in Victoria, British Columbia (2014), 127.
20. Sovereign Grand Lodge of the Independent Order of Odd Fellows, Journal of Proceedings of the One Hundred and Sixty-Sixth Annual Communication of the Sovereign Grand Lodge I.O.O.F (1993), (Volume LXXX) (Winston-Salem: The Sovereign Grand Lodge of the I.O.O.F., 1994), 390.
21. Sovereign Grand Lodge of the Independent Order of Odd Fellows, Journal of Proceedings of the One Hundred and Seventy-Fifth Annual Communication of the Sovereign Grand Lodge I.O.O.F (2001), (Volume LXXXXIX) (Winston-Salem: The Sovereign Grand Lodge of the I.O.O.F., 2002), 20.
22. Annual Report of Grand Ladies Encampment Auxiliaries to The Sovereign Grand Lodge, I.O.O.F ending December 31, 2018.

III. Encampment Degrees, Teachings and Symbols
1. J. Powley, Concise History of Odd Fellowship, 37.
2. Ibid.
3. Sovereign Grand Lodge of the Independent Order of Odd Fellows, Journal of Proceedings of the Right Worthy Grand Lodge of the United States, from its formation in February, 1879-1881 (Volume X) (Baltimore: Sovereign Grand Lodge I.O.O.F (1887), 8674.
4. Ibid.
5. Ibid.
6. Regulations, Charges, and Lectures of the Patriarchal Order as adopted by

the Grand Lodge of the United States of the Independent Order of Odd Fellows (Baltimore: Grand Lodge of the United States, 1849).
7. Rev. A.B. Grosh, The Odd Fellows Manual, 269.
8. J. Powley, Concise History of Odd Fellowship, 38.
9. J. Powley, Concise History of Odd Fellowship, 29.
10. Ibid.
11. Ibid.
12. Ibid.
13. Ibid, 13.
14. Ibid.
15. Theo A. Ross, The History and Manual of Odd Fellowship, 473.
16. Ibid.
17. Ibid.
18. Ibid.
19. Ibid.
20. Ritual of the Patriarchal Degree, The Sovereign Grand Lodge of the Independent Order of Odd Fellows (n.d.)
21. Rev. Benson Mahlon Powell, The Triple Links, 207-209.
22. Ibid.
23. Ibid.
24. Ibid.
25. Rev. A.B. Grosh, The Odd Fellows Manual, 271.
26. Ibid.
27. Rev. Benson Mahlon Powell, The Triple Links, 207-209.
28. Ibid, 11.
29. Ibid.
30. J. Powley, Concise History of Odd Fellowship, 35.
31. Ritual of the Golden Rule Degree, The Sovereign Grand Lodge of the Independent Order of Odd Fellows (n.d.)
32. Ibid.
33. Ibid.
34. Theo A. Ross, The History and Manual of Odd Fellowship, 474.
35. Ibid.
36. Rev. A.B. Grosh, The Odd Fellows Manual, 280-281.
37. Rev. Benson Mahlon Powell, The Triple Links, 215-216.
38. Ibid.
39. Ibid.
40. Ibid, 12.
41. Ibid.
42. J. Powley, Concise History of Odd Fellowship, 35.

43. The Triple Links, 220-224
44. Ibid.
45. Ritual of the Royal Purple Degree, The Sovereign Grand Lodge of the Independent Order of Odd Fellows (n.d.)
46. Ibid.
47. Rev. A.B. Grosh, The Odd Fellows Manual, 293.
48. Rev. Benson Mahlon Powell, The Triple Links, 220-224
49. Ibid.
50. Rev. A.B. Grosh, The Odd Fellows Manual, 293.

IV. Regalia
1. Sovereign Grand Lodge of the Independent Order of Odd Fellows, Journal of Proceedings of the Right Worthy Grand Lodge of the United States, from its formation in February, 1821-1846 (Volume I) (Baltimore: Sovereign Grand Lodge I.O.O.F (1893), 20.
2. Rev. A.B. Grosh, The Odd Fellows Manual, 268.
3. Sovereign Grand Lodge of the Independent Order of Odd Fellows, Journal of Proceedings of the Right Worthy Grand Lodge of the United States, from its formation in February, 1879-1881 (Volume X) (Baltimore: Sovereign Grand Lodge I.O.O.F (1893), 8050.
4. Ibid.
5. Sovereign Grand Lodge of the Independent Order of Odd Fellows, Journal of Proceedings of the Right Worthy Grand Lodge of the United States, from its formation in February, 1821-1846 (Volume I) (Baltimore: Sovereign Grand Lodge I.O.O.F (1893), 20.

V. Encampment and its Officers
1. Sovereign Grand Lodge of the Independent Order of Odd Fellows, Journal of Proceedings of the One Hundred and Sixty-Ninth Annual Communication of the Sovereign Grand Lodge I.O.O.F (1995), (Volume LXXXIII) (Winston-Salem: The Sovereign Grand Lodge of the I.O.O.F., 1996), 305.
2. Ibid.
3. Code of General Laws of The Sovereign Grand Lodge I.O.O.F. (2017).
4. Ibid.
5. Ibid.
6. Ibid.
7. Ibid.
8. Ibid.
9. Ibid.

10. Ibid.
11. Ibid.

Elective Officers
1. Rev. A.B. Grosh, The Odd Fellows Manual, 264-311.
2. Ibid.
3. Ibid.

Appointive Officers
1. Ibid.

VI. Grand Encampment and its Officers
1. Nathan Billstein, A Brief History of The Encampment Branch of the I.O.O.F. and A Statement of Its Accomplishments and Aims, 13.
2. Ibid.
3. Rev. A.B. Grosh, The Odd Fellows Manual, 303-311.
4. Ibid.
5. Code of General Laws of The Sovereign Grand Lodge I.O.O.F. (2017), 239.
6. Ibid.
7. Ibid.
8. Ibid.
9. Code of General Laws of The Sovereign Grand Lodge I.O.O.F. (2017), 253.
10. Ibid.

Elective Officers
1. Rev. A.B. Grosh, The Odd Fellows Manual, 310.
2. Ibid.
3. Ibid.

References

A. Published Books

Andrews. *Thomas The Jericho Road: The Philosophy of Odd Fellowship*. Oklahoma: The William Thomas Co., 1937.

Beharrell, Thomas. *The Brotherhood: Being a Presentation of Odd Fellowship*. Indiana: Brotherhood Publishing Co., 1875.

Beharrell, Thomas. *Odd Fellows Monitor and Guide*. Indianapolis: Robert Douglass, 1883.

Beharrell, Thomas. *The Brotherhood: Being a Presentation of Odd Fellowship*. Indiana: Brotherhood Publishing Co., 1875.

Billstein, Nathan. *One Hundred Years of Patriarchal Odd Fellowship*. Baltimore: Nathan Billstein, 1927.

Brooks, Charles H. *The Official History and Manual of the Grand United Order of Odd Fellows in America: A chronological Treatise*. Philadelphia, Odd Fellows Journal Print, 1902.

Curry, Elvin James. *The Red Blood of Odd Fellowship*. Maryland: Elvin Curry, 1903.

Donaldson, Paschal. *The Odd Fellows Text Book*. Philadelphia: Moss & Brother, 1852.

Donaldson, Paschal. *The Odd Fellows' Pocket Companion*. Ohio: R.W. Carroll & Co, 1881.

Grosh, Aaron Burt. *The Odd Fellows Manual*. Philadelphia: H.C. Peck and Theo Bliss, 1852.

Grosh, Aaron Burt. *The Odd Fellow's Manual*. Philadelphia: H.C. Peck & Theo Bliss, 1860.

Grosh, Aaron Burt. *The Odd-Fellows Improved Pocket Manual*. New York: Clark & Maynard, 1873.

Grosh, Aaron Burt. *A Manual of Odd Fellowship. New York*: New York: Clark & Maynard, 1882.

Powell, Rev. Benson Mahlon. *The Triple Links*. Kansas: ED. G. Moore & Son, 1900.

Powley, Joseph. *Concise History of Odd Fellowship*. Toronto: The Grand Lodge of Ontario IOOF, 1943.

Powley, Joseph. *Concise History of Odd Fellowship (Revised edition)*. Toronto: Macoomb Publishing, 1952.

Ridgely, James Lot. *History of American Odd Fellowship: The First Decade*. Baltimore: James Lot Ridgely, 1878.

Ross, Theodore. *Odd Fellowship: Its History and Manual*. New York: M.W. Hazen Co., 1888.

Ross, Theo A. *The History and Manual of Odd Fellowship*. New York: The M.W. Hazen Company, 1900.

Stillson, Henry Leonard. *The Official History of Odd Fellowship*. Boston: The Fraternity Publishing Company, 1990.

Stillson, Henry Leonard. *The Official History of Odd Fellowship*. Massachusetts: Fraternity Publishing Company, 1908.

Wallace, W.W. *The Odd-Fellows' Keepsake: A Concise History of Odd-Fellowship in the United States*. New York: Office of the Mirror of the Times, 1850.

B. Journal of Proceedings

Sovereign Grand Lodge of the Independent Order of Odd Fellows. *Journal of Proceedings of the Right Worthy Grand Lodge of the United States, from its formation in February, 1821-1846 (Volume I)*. Baltimore: Sovereign Grand Lodge I.O.O.F, 1893.

Sovereign Grand Lodge of the Independent Order of Odd Fellows. *Journal of Proceedings of the Right Worthy Grand Lodge of the United States, from its formation in February, 1879-1881 (Volume X)*. Baltimore: Sovereign Grand Lodge I.O.O.F, 1887.

Sovereign Grand Lodge of the Independent Order of Odd Fellows, *Journal of Proceedings of the One Hundred and Sixty-Sixth Annual Communication of the Sovereign Grand Lodge I.O.O.F, 1993* (Volume LXXX). Winston-Salem: The Sovereign Grand

Lodge of the I.O.O.F., 1994.

Sovereign Grand Lodge of the Independent Order of Odd Fellows, *Journal of Proceedings of the One Hundred and Sixty-Ninth Annual Communication of the Sovereign Grand Lodge I.O.O.F, 1995,* (Volume LXXXIII). Winston-Salem: The Sovereign Grand Lodge of the I.O.O.F., 1996.

Sovereign Grand Lodge of the Independent Order of Odd Fellows, *Journal of Proceedings of the One Hundred and Seventy-Fifth Annual Communication of the Sovereign Grand Lodge I.O.O.F., 2001,* (Volume LXXXXIX). Winston-Salem: The Sovereign Grand Lodge of the I.O.O.F., 2002.

C. Rituals

Charge Book for an Encampment under the Jurisdiction of The Sovereign Grand Lodge of the Independent Order of Odd Fellows. Winston-Salem: The Sovereign Grand Lodge, IOOF, 1996.

Regulations, Charges, and Lectures of the Patriarchal Order as adopted by the Grand Lodge of the United States of the Independent Order of Odd Fellows. Baltimore: Grand Lodge of the United States, 1849.

Ritual of the Loyal and Ancient Order of Odd Fellows, 1805.

Ritual of the Independent Order of Odd Fellows Manchester Unity Friendly Society for the Use of District Officers. Manchester: Manchester Unity IOOF, 1989.

Ritual of a Subordinate Encampment under the Jurisdiction of The Sovereign Grand Lodge of the Independent Order of Odd Fellows. Baltimore: The Sovereign Grand Lodge, I.O.O.F., 1944.

Ritual of the Patriarchal Degree, The Sovereign Grand Lodge of the Independent Order of Odd Fellows

Ritual of the Golden Rule Degree, The Sovereign Grand Lodge of the Independent Order of Odd Fellows

Ritual of the Royal Purple Degree, The Sovereign Grand Lodge of the Independent Order of Odd Fellows

Supplement to the Lecture Book of the Manchester Unity of the Independent Order of Odd Fellows. Manchester: P.G.M. Mark Wardle, 1834.

D. Others

Advance Reports of the Officers and Committees of The Sovereign Grand Lodge Independent Order of Odd Fellows Held in Victoria, British Columbia, 2014.

Annual Report of Grand Encampments to The Sovereign Grand Lodge, I.O.O.F ending December 31, 1927.

Annual Report of Grand Encampments to The Sovereign Grand Lodge, I.O.O.F ending December 31, 2018.

Annual Report of Grand Ladies Encampment Auxiliaries to The Sovereign Grand Lodge, I.O.O.F ending December 31, 2018.

Code of General Laws of The Sovereign Grand Lodge I.O.O.F., 2017.

In Faith, Hope & Charity